PERU
the land

Bobbie Kalman & David Schimpky

The Lands, Peoples, and Cultures Series

Crabtree Publishing Company

Toronto · Oxford · New York

The Lands, Peoples, and Cultures Series
Created by Bobbie Kalman

For Michael Vaughan

Editor-in-Chief
Bobbie Kalman

Writing team
Bobbie Kalman
David Schimpky

Editors
Tammy Everts
Petrina Gentile
Lynda Hale
Janine Schaub
David Schimpky

Consultant
Ronald Wright, author of *Cut Stones
and Crossroads, A Journey in Peru*
(Viking Penguin, 1984)

Computer design
Lynda Hale

Separations and film
Book Art Inc.

Printer
Worzalla Publishing Company

Special thanks to
Federico Perez Eguren, Eco Expeditions; Pierre Vachon, CIDA;
Antonio Saer, Consulate of Peru

Photographs
Jim Bryant: title page, pages 7 (bottom), 11, 12 (inset), 13, 17 (both),
18 (both), 20 (both), 21 (top right, bottom right), 22 (inset), 24 (inset),
25, 26, 28, 29 (bottom), 30 (middle, bottom)
Eco Expeditions: pages 5, 6 (bottom left), 27 (both)
James Kamstra: page 15 (bottom left)
Joe Langer/Pacific Rim Slide Bank: cover
Donna Maher/Pacific Rim Slide Bank: page 10 (top)
Pat Morrow/CIDA: pages 8, 10 (bottom), 12
Denis Nervig/Fowler Museum of Cultural History: pages 6 (bottom right), 7 (top)
Inga Spence/Tom Stack & Associates: page 14 (bottom)
Ellen Tolmie/CIDA: page 10 (middle)
Robert Tymstra: pages 14-15, 15 (bottom right), 19, 24, 29 (top, inset), 30 (top)
Elias Wakan/Pacific Rim Slide Bank: pages 3, 9, 21 (left), 22, 23

Illustrations
Barb Bedell: back cover
Antoinette "Cookie" DeBiasi: page 8
Rudy Irish: page 16

The ancient city of Machu Picchu is shown on the cover. The title page shows
dugout canoes on the shore of a river in the Peruvian rainforest. The golden
ear ornament on the back cover is similar to those made by Moche artisans.

Published by
Crabtree Publishing Company

350 Fifth Avenue	360 York Road, RR 4,	73 Lime Walk
Suite 3308	Niagara-on-the-Lake,	Headington
New York	Ontario, Canada	Oxford OX3 7AD
N.Y. 10118	L0S 1J0	United Kingdom

Cataloging in Publication Data
Kalman, Bobbie, 1947-
  Peru: the land

(Lands, Peoples, and Cultures Series)
Includes index.
ISBN 0-86505-221-2 (library bound)   ISBN 0-86505-301-4 (pbk.)
This book examines the history, geography, natural resources,
agriculture, and transportation systems of Peru.

1. Peru - Description and travel - Juvenile literature.
I. Schimpky, David, 1969-   . II. Title. III. Series.

F3408.5.K34 1994   j985   LC 94-874

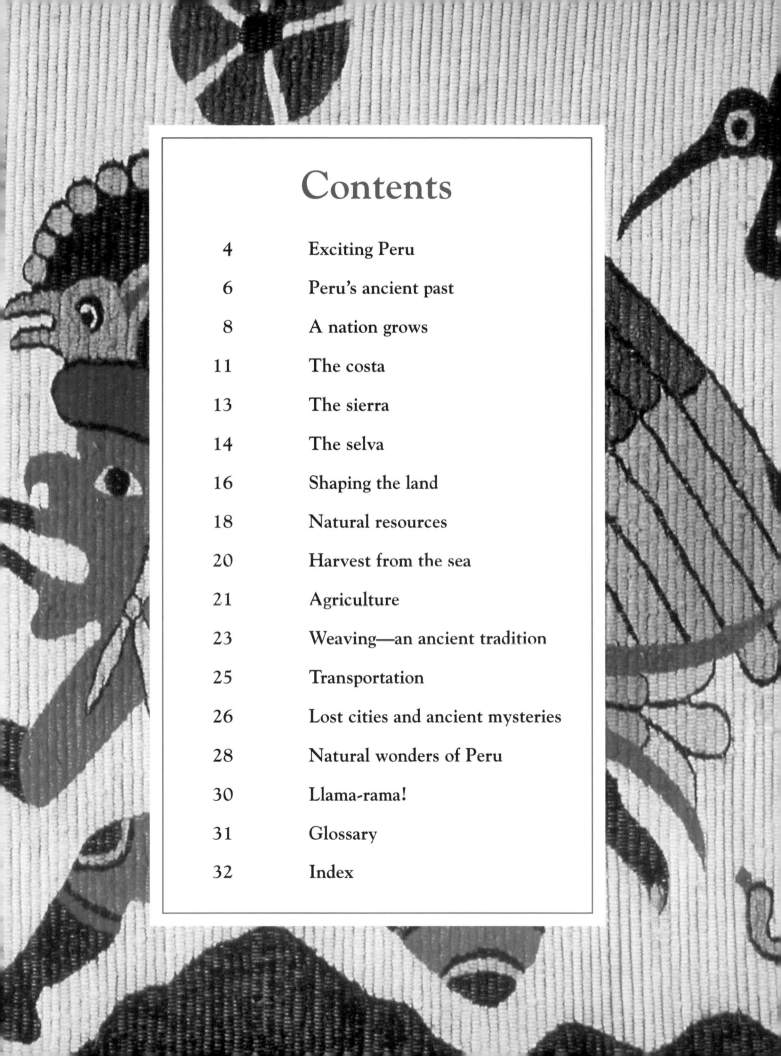

Contents

4   Exciting Peru

6   Peru's ancient past

8   A nation grows

11   The costa

13   The sierra

14   The selva

16   Shaping the land

18   Natural resources

20   Harvest from the sea

21   Agriculture

23   Weaving—an ancient tradition

25   Transportation

26   Lost cities and ancient mysteries

28   Natural wonders of Peru

30   Llama-rama!

31   Glossary

32   Index

🦙 Exciting Peru 🦙

Peru is an exciting country. Its colorful history is thousands of years old. The landscape of Peru includes breathtaking mountain peaks, flat desert areas, and rich tropical rainforest. Bustling modern cities, quiet rural villages, and majestic ancient ruins are also part of Peru.

Take a journey back in time and visit the fabulous cities built by the Incas! Climb the high peaks of the Andes Mountains and explore the wonders of the rainforest! Meet the friendly Peruvians and get to know a llama! These adventures await you. Turn the page!

Facts at a glance:

Official name: Republic of Peru
Capital city: Lima
Population: 22,454,000 (1992)
Area: 1,285,220 square kilometers
      (496,262 square miles)
Official languages: Spanish and Quechua
Main religion: Roman Catholic
Currency: New sol (100 centavos)
National holiday: Independence Day (July 28)

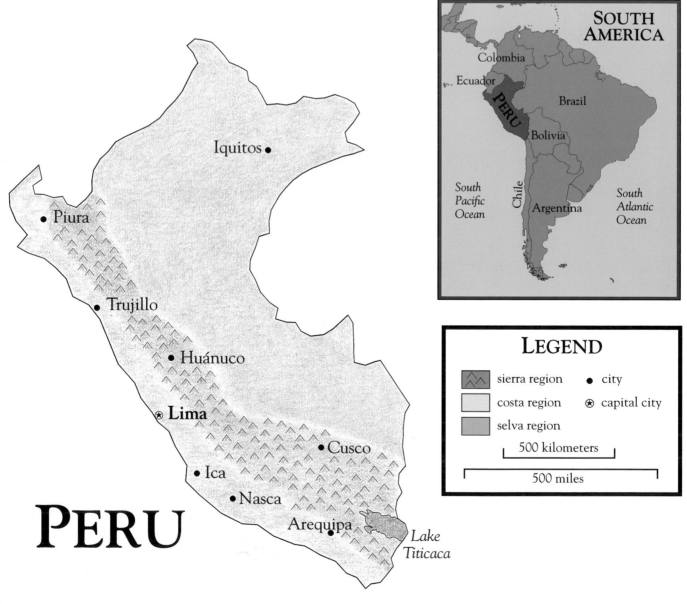

LEGEND

⋀⋀ sierra region		● city
☐ costa region		⊛ capital city
▨ selva region		

500 kilometers

500 miles

Peru's climate

Peru is located just south of the **equator**, an imaginary line around the earth that is at equal distances from the north and south poles. Areas near the equator have **tropical** climates—warm weather year round, with dry and rainy seasons. South of the equator the dry season is from May to September. The rainy season, when crops grow, is from October to April.

Peru is considered a tropical country, but its climate varies from region to region. A cold ocean current in the waters off Peru produces mild weather along the coast. This area receives very little rain. Mountain areas are so high that they experience cool, windy weather and a great deal of sunshine. The huge rainforest in the east is the only part of Peru that has true tropical weather.

Peru has been the home of many great **civilizations** of ancient peoples who were skilled in arts and sciences. Most of our knowledge about the history of ancient Peru has come from the discoveries of **archaeologists**. Archaeologists study artifacts, such as pottery or statues, and architecture to find out about the past. The ancient peoples of Peru did not have written languages, so studying the objects they left behind is the only way to learn about their lives.

The timeline below shows when each civilization flourished. For more information on each civilization, refer to the box of the same color.

The Chavín

The Chavín civilization was the first great culture in Peru. The Chavín had strong religious beliefs. Their temples were decorated with sculptures of jaguars, eagles, and snakes. These symbols have been found on ruins across the mountain and coastal regions of Peru. This makes archaeologists believe that the Chavín religion influenced many ancient peoples in Peru.

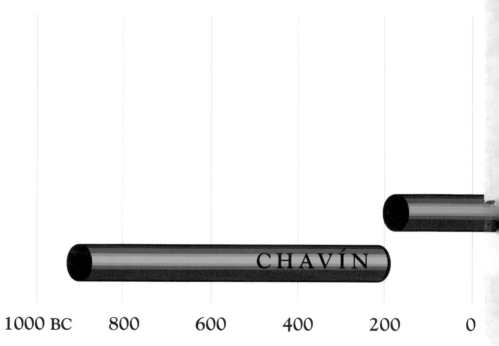

CHAVÍN

| 1000 BC | 800 | 600 | 400 | 200 | 0 |

The Nascas

The Nasca civilization flourished on Peru's coast between 200 BC and AD 500. The Nascas are most famous for the huge pictures of spiders, dogs, and birds they etched in the desert near the modern city of Ica. The designs are so large that the best way to view them is from an airplane high in the sky! (See additional photographs on page 27.)

The Moche

The Moche civilization was powerful from AD 100 to 800. The Moche, who lived in northern Peru, fought and conquered many neighboring peoples. They built huge cities that were connected by a network of roads. Moche arts included realistic sculptures of people.

The Huari

The Huari were a powerful Native group that lived near what is now the city of Ayacucho. Archaeologists believe that the Huari empire spread quickly over much of Peru and may have been responsible for the decline of the Moche civilization. The Huari civilization collapsed suddenly around AD 1000. Its cities were abandoned and fell into ruin.

The Chimú

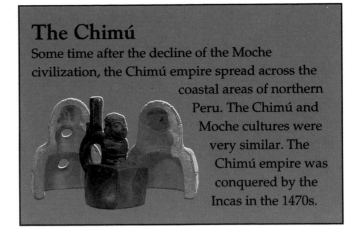

Some time after the decline of the Moche civilization, the Chimú empire spread across the coastal areas of northern Peru. The Chimú and Moche cultures were very similar. The Chimú empire was conquered by the Incas in the 1470s.

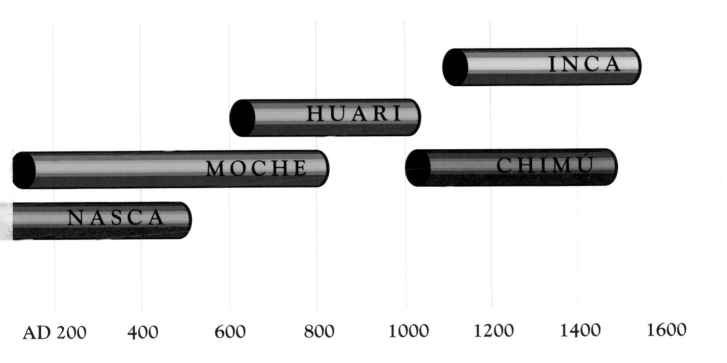

INCA

HUARI

MOCHE

CHIMÚ

NASCA

AD 200   400   600   800   1000   1200   1400   1600

The powerful Incas

The most famous civilization in Peru was the Inca empire, which stretched across much of South America's west coast. The civilization began in the 1100s and, by the 1400s, it was a highly organized society. A powerful emperor controlled the state from the mountain city of Cusco.

The mountain city of Machu Picchu was an Inca refuge during the Spanish invasion.

Francisco Pizarro landed in northern Peru with a band of soldiers. They killed Atahualpa and many of his followers. The Spanish then moved south and conquered more of the Inca empire. The Incas fought bravely, but the Spanish pushed them further into the mountains of southern Peru. During this time, many Incas died from smallpox,

In 1532 two brothers, Atahualpa and Huáscar, fought over the Inca throne. Atahualpa, a skilled general, was close to victory when a Spaniard named a disease brought to Peru by the Spanish. By 1572, the Spanish controlled all of what was once the Inca empire.

A nation grows

For nearly 300 years the Spanish controlled Peru. Native Peruvians fought to regain their freedom in 1780, when Tupac Amaru II, a descendant of the last Inca king, tried to restore Inca rule. The Incas were defeated by the Spanish rulers. In the 1820s, Peruvians again revolted. This time they were aided by troops from Argentina that were led by General José de San Martín and by the army of Simón Bolívar. In 1826 the last Spanish troops in Peru surrendered, and Peru's white minority gained control of the country.

Years of conflict

The young nation faced many difficulties during the next 50 years, including severe poverty and wars with neighboring nations. Near the end of the nineteenth century, foreign companies controlled much of Peru's natural resources. These companies developed new industries, but they did not help the majority of Peruvians. Most of Peru's wealth was held by just a few people.

Government difficulties

Although Peru is supposed to be governed by elected leaders, there were times when there were no free elections. The army controlled the government from 1949 to 1956 and from 1968 to 1980. People were not allowed to vote during these periods. Since 1980, however, Peruvians have been able to elect their leaders. The biggest problems the government now faces are poverty, unemployment, terrorism, and crime.

A troubled economy

You have probably heard the word "economy" used by your parents. A country's **economy** is the organization and management of its money, businesses, and industries. For many years Peru has had a troubled economy. Part of the problem is Peru's **national debt**. The government has borrowed large amounts of money from other countries. It must use much of its income to pay the borrowing fees, called **interest**. This means

(above) Simón Bolívar, a general from Venezuela, helped many South American countries gain independence. (below) Guards in ceremonial uniforms protect the Government Palace in Lima.

the government cannot use its tax money to help businesses grow or to build roads, schools, or hospitals.

Foreign help

The government of Peru is trying to improve the economy by attracting foreign businesses and industries. Some people hope that these companies will provide jobs for Peruvians and bring much-needed money into the country.

The Shining Path

The Shining Path is a **terrorist** group that operates in Peru. Terrorists are people who try to achieve their political goals by using violence. The Shining Path was formed in the mountain city of Ayacucho in 1980. For years it has fought to overthrow the government of Peru with bombings and murders. The government is harsh in its attempts to stop the Shining Path. Innocent people are often caught in the middle. If they side with the government, the Shining Path may harm them or their families, and if they side with the Shining Path, they may face going to jail.

Law and order

Crime is a serious problem in Peru. Some unemployed Peruvians resort to stealing to make money. Thieves and pickpockets rob tourists in the big cities. Some wealthy families have built large walls around their homes for protection from robbers. In parts of Peru, the drug trade is a big business, and the drug dealers sometimes bribe the police. Many honest police officers, however, are battling the drug problem.

Looking to the future

Peruvians are working together to create a better future. Terrorist groups have been losing strength, and violence is declining. Peru's government is making an effort to pay back its large foreign debt. With its many hardworking citizens and a wealth of natural resources, Peru is sure to overcome the challenges it faces.

Productive cotton farms are an important part of Peru's economy.

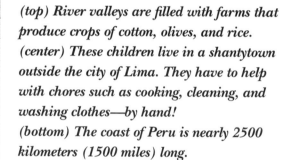

(top) River valleys are filled with farms that produce crops of cotton, olives, and rice.
(center) These children live in a shantytown outside the city of Lima. They have to help with chores such as cooking, cleaning, and washing clothes—by hand!
(bottom) The coast of Peru is nearly 2500 kilometers (1500 miles) long.

 The costa

Peru has three geographic regions: the **costa**, the **sierra**, and the **selva**. The costa, or coastal region, of Peru is a narrow strip along the country's coast. It is bordered by the Pacific Ocean on the west and the Andes Mountains on the east. The landscape includes flat plains, shifting sand dunes, rough hills, and a few trees. This desert area receives less rain than the Sahara!

Green in the desert

The many rivers that run through the costa begin high in the Andes Mountains and flow into the Pacific Ocean. The valleys around the rivers are fertile areas called **oases**. Cotton, sugar cane, olives, rice, and fruit are among the agricultural products that grow in the oases.

Strange weather

The costa experiences unusual weather. The coast is a desert because of the influence of the **Humboldt Current**. This cold ocean current from Antarctica flows by Peru's coast. When the wind blows over the water, the air is cool and water cannot evaporate. As a result, Peru's coast receives little rain. From October to June, however, some water evaporates. As the moist air reaches the coast, it sits over the costa, causing fog and drizzle called *garúa*.

El Niño

About every twenty years, Peru experiences a huge change in the weather. A warm ocean current called **El Niño** flows south from the equator. The warm water kills most of the fish that live in Peru's normally cold coastal waters. The fishing industry suffers great losses. Thousands of birds that eat the fish starve. The warm water also causes tropical storms, which bring heavy rain, floods, and mudslides. In 1982, El Niño was responsible for the deaths of 600 people in Ecuador and Peru.

Lima

Most of Peru's large cities, including Lima, the capital, are located in the costa. Lima is the financial and political center of Peru. The nation's most important port, Callao, is located right next to this large city. More than six million people live in Lima. Many cannot afford good homes and live in the slums and shantytowns that surround the city. Most of these areas lack clean water, sewers, electricity, and medical facilities.

(above) Sea lions enjoy the cold coastal waters of Peru. The **Humboldt Current** *brings the chilly water past Peru as it flows north from Antarctica.*

11

🦙 The sierra 🦙

Although the sun is shining brightly, the air is cold. A lone condor soars above you in the clear sky. Every few minutes you take a break to catch your breath—you are so high in the mountains that there is little oxygen. Finally, you reach the top of the mountain. The view is amazing. You can see distant mountain ranges, valleys, alpine lakes, glaciers, and plateaus. Now you know why people say the Andes is one of the world's most spectacular mountain ranges!

A land of variety

The **sierra** region, made up of the Andes Mountains, stretches from north to south through the middle of Peru. The western and eastern slopes of the sierra are very different. The western slopes border the deserts of the costa and are hit by constant dry winds. The eastern slopes, on the other hand, border the Amazon rainforest and experience warm, humid weather.

The area between the eastern and western edges of the sierra is filled with hills, valleys, forests, canyons, and plateaus. Clear mountain lakes and roaring rivers can be found throughout this region. A vast, high-altitude plain called the Altiplano stretches across southern Peru and the neighboring country of Bolivia.

The Cordillera Blanca

The Andes Mountains are actually a combination of several small mountain ranges. The Cordillera Blanca is the most magnificent range in Peru. It contains Peru's tallest mountain, Huascarán. This 6770-meter (22,210-foot) peak is located in Huascarán National Park, one of Peru's first national parks. The park's purpose is to protect the natural beauty of the land around this famous mountain.

(opposite page) The eastern slopes of the Andes, near the rainforest, are covered with thick vegetation.
(opposite page, inset) Native Peruvians use the llama as a pack animal and a source of wool and meat.

(above) Cusco is one of the most famous cities in Peru. Many building foundations were constructed when this mountain city was the capital of the Inca empire.

Mountain sickness

Many people who visit the Andes experience *soroche*, or altitude sickness. In high-altitude areas there is less oxygen in the air than at lower altitudes. As a result, when people inhale, they take less oxygen into their bodies than they are used to breathing in. People with *soroche* get tired very easily and experience headaches, dizziness, and upset stomach. The best cure is several days of rest.

Over centuries, the bodies of the Native peoples have adapted to the air at high altitudes. They take frequent breaths, and their bodies have more red blood cells to carry oxygen in their blood. Scientists once believed that the Native peoples had larger hearts and lungs than people who live at lower altitudes. Now researchers feel that, in time, anyone can adapt to a high altitude.

🦙 The selva 🦙

East of the sierra is a world of dense forests filled with a rich variety of plants and animals. This region is called the **selva**, and it is part of the vast Amazon rainforest.

Unique plants

The forests of the selva are called "rainforests" because they receive a great deal of rain. The continual rains, along with warm temperatures, allow unique plant species to live in these forests. This plant life exists in layers. At the top is a thick layer of treetops called the **canopy**. Beneath this layer is an **understory** of shorter trees, vines, and other plants. The floor of the rainforest is covered with mosses and small plants.

Amazing animals

Thousands of animal species live in the rainforest, too. A wide variety of insects, such as ants, beetles, and butterflies, can be found there. Monkeys and sloths dwell in the canopy and understory. Jaguars, tapirs, lizards, and countless other animals live on the ground. The forest is also home to Peru's largest animal—the anaconda, a giant snake that can grow up to 10 meters (33 feet) long!

Cloudforests

A **cloudforest** is a special kind of rainforest that is located in the hilly selva areas near the Andes. Instead of receiving heavy rainfall, cloudforests are continually covered by mist and fog. The weather is cool and the vegetation thick and low.

The people of the selva

Few people live in the selva. Native groups inhabited the area long before Europeans arrived in South America. Some still dwell in remote parts of the rainforest and carry on the ways of their ancestors. Recently, settlers have moved into the selva, clearing forests to create farmland. Employees of oil and logging companies have also built homes in the selva.

Iquitos

Iquitos is the largest city in the selva. It was just a small town until the late 1800s, when the rubber industry turned it into an important city. The rubber trees in the nearby rainforest were the source of the sap needed to make rubber. Many Native peoples were enslaved during the rubber boom. As rubber trees were planted in other parts of the world, money stopped flowing into Iquitos. Today Iquitos is a popular base for tourists who want to visit the rainforest. The city is also a center for oil and logging businesses.

Changing the selva

Rainforests have taken centuries to develop. If a rainforest ecosystem is destroyed, it may never recover. Peru's rainforests have not experienced the destruction that rainforests have in other parts of the world, but logging, oil drilling, farming, and tourism are changing the selva. As more people move into the area and forests are cut down, there is less room for plants and animals. Many rainforest species are nearly extinct. The traditional ways of the Native peoples are also threatened.

(top) The lush rainforest is a threatened ecosystem.
(left, inset) The jaguar is an endangered animal because of hunting and habitat destruction.
(right, inset) The harpy eagle is the largest bird of prey in the rainforest. Harpy eagles sometimes eat monkeys!
(opposite page, inset) The Yagua people maintain a traditional way of life in Peru's rainforest.

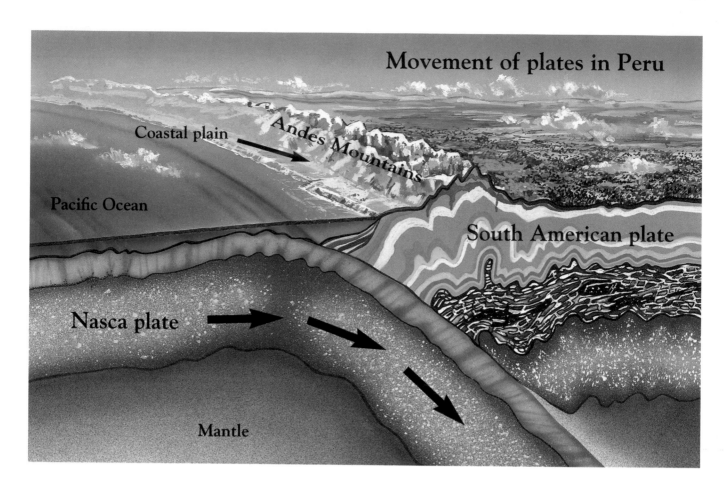

Movement of plates in Peru

Coastal plain

Andes Mountains

Pacific Ocean

South American plate

Nasca plate

Mantle

🦙 Shaping the land 🦙

Peru has experienced many earthquakes and some volcanic activity in its history. The Inca word for earthquake, *pachakuti*, means "world overturning." The Incas believed that turning points in history, such as conquests and wars, resembled great earthquakes. The first Inca emperor took *Pachakuti* as his name.

Plate tectonics

A theory called **plate tectonics** explains why earthquakes occur and how mountains and volcanoes are formed. Scientists believe that the earth is composed of three layers. At the center of the earth is the **core**. Around the core is the thick **mantle**. The thin surface of the earth is called the **crust**. It is divided into several large pieces called **plates**. The plates are constantly moving. Some move toward one another, others move away from one another, and still others rub sideways against one another.

The earth moves

On the western coast of South America, the Nasca plate collides with and is pushed beneath the South American plate. The force of the collision has pushed up huge amounts of rock, creating the Andes Mountains—the world's second-highest mountain range.

The movement of the plates is usually very slow, but sometimes the plates suddenly shift. Shock waves called **tremors** shake the crust. Severe shaking is called an **earthquake**. Earthquakes have troubled Peru for centuries. In 1950 an earthquake destroyed much of the city of Cusco.

(above) This diagram shows what happens beneath the earth as the Nasca plate pushes against the South American plate. Parts of the South American plate have been crumpled by the collision, creating the tall peaks of the Andes Mountains.

(above) In 1970 an earthquake shook Huascarán, Peru's highest mountain. A huge avalanche of ice and rock slid down the mountain, burying surrounding areas, including the town of Yungay. Nearly 80,000 people died. (below) Massive chunks of rock are forced up when plates collide, creating tall mountain peaks.

Birth of a volcano

Volcanoes are another result of plate movements. Large amounts of rock are pushed into the mantle where the Nasca plate hits the South American plate. The temperature inside the mantle is very high, and the rock melts and rises to the crust. In places where there are cracks in the crust, the melted rock, called **magma**, flows up to the surface of the earth. When the magma reaches the air, it is called **lava**. As the lava cools and hardens, it builds up and forms a high cone.

Eruption!

Sometimes the hardened lava seals the volcano. The pressure from rising magma, along with gas and steam, can cause an explosion called an **eruption**. The largest volcano in Peru, El Misti, last erupted in 1869. Today it releases just steam and ash.

Natural resources

Peru is a country rich in **natural resources**. Natural resources are substances found in nature that are used by people. Minerals, trees, oil, and water are natural resources.

Logging

Logging has been a money-making business in Peru for decades. In some areas, large sections of forest are cleared until not one tree remains standing! Some areas are logged only for valuable trees, such as cedar and mahogany. Much of Peru's rainforest has escaped heavy logging because it is too expensive to transport the wood over the mountains. Many mountain forests, however, have been cut down.

Preserving the forests

In parts of Peru's rainforest, Native peoples are experimenting with a new logging method that does not harm the rainforest permanently. It is called the **strip-shelterbelt system**. Strips 27 meters (88 feet) wide are cut and cleared from the forest. The rainforest ecosystem is able to recover within 35 years.

Minerals in the mountains

Minerals such as copper, iron, silver, and manganese are taken from mines located high in the Andes Mountains. At the high altitude, there is little oxygen in the air. Workers from lower altitudes find breathing difficult, so most mining companies hire local Native people who are accustomed to the mountain air.

Gold in the jungle

For centuries Peru has attracted adventurers in search of gold. The first gold-seekers were the Spanish, who took huge amounts of gold from the Incas. Today, people search for gold dust and nuggets in the rivers and streams of Peru's rainforest. Temporary "cities" of prospectors have sprung up in remote rainforest areas.

Oil wells

Oil companies have discovered large oil deposits in Peru. The first oil wells were located in the northern deserts. Recently, many wells have been drilled in the northern parts of the rainforest. The oil is transported to the coast through pipelines that cross the mountains.

An unusual resource

Peru has one natural resource that many people might consider unusual. It is **guano**, or bird droppings! The guanay is a type of seabird that lives on Peru's coast. For thousands of years its droppings piled up on islands. The Incas used small amounts as fertilizer. During the nineteenth century, guano was harvested and sold for high prices. Today, guano harvests are much smaller. Heavy fishing in the coastal waters has reduced the population of anchovies, the main food of the guanay. This once-plentiful seabird may soon become an endangered species.

*(right) Oil refineries transform **crude oil**, or oil straight from the ground, into **refined oil**, which is used as fuel.*
(opposite page, top) A century ago, the droppings of the guanay were among Peru's major exports.
(opposite page, bottom) The easiest way to transport logs in the selva is to float them down rivers.

Fishing is an important industry in Peru. The cold waters off the coast are rich fishing grounds because of tiny creatures called **plankton**. Plankton, which live in cold ocean water, are food for a wide variety of ocean life.

An ancient tradition

Long before the Spanish conquered Peru, Native peoples fished in the ocean and in the waters of Lake Titicaca. Fishers used boats that were constructed by lashing together many reeds. Fish was an important part of the Inca diet. If the Inca emperor, who lived in the mountains, desired a seafood dinner, runners delivered fish from the coast within two days!

Big business

In the 1960s, fishing became a huge industry in Peru. Until recently, large modern fishing boats hauled in nets full of anchovies. These tiny fish are dried and ground up to make **fishmeal**. Fishmeal is an important cattle feed because it is full of protein.

Unfortunately, overfishing has caused anchovy numbers to decline. In an effort to help the schools recover, anchovy fishing is now regulated. Fishing is still an important industry in Peru, and many fishing crews catch swordfish, bonito, tuna, shrimp, and crab. Fish such as sole and Pacific snapper are sold to other countries.

(above) Some fishing folk who live on Peru's coast use traditional reed boats called **caballitos**. **Caballito** *means "little horse" in Spanish. People sit on the boats in the same way they would ride a horse.*
(inset) Fishing crews on Lake Titicaca use sailboats to take advantage of the strong breezes.

🦙 Agriculture 🦙

Until the 1960s, a few wealthy families owned vast farms, called *haciendas*. They hired Native people to work for them. The workers were paid little or no money, but they received a place to live and a small plot of land for growing vegetables. In the 1970s the government passed laws to stop this type of farming. Now the people who work the land also own it and share the profits. Some of these farms, called **cooperatives**, are successful, but many are not as efficient as the *haciendas* were.

Farming in the regions

In the costa region, most farmland is located in the river valleys. These farms rely on irrigation to bring water to the dry land. Cotton and sugar cane are grown there. They are called **cash crops** because they are grown to be **exported**, or sold to other countries. The rice, corn, fruit, and olives grown in this region are sold within Peru.

The land in the sierra is not very good for large-scale farming, but potatoes, corn, and grains are among the traditional crops that thrive there. Livestock graze in mountain pastures.

The hilly parts of the selva between the Andes Mountains and the rainforest are excellent for growing coffee beans. Over the last twenty years, Peru's coffee farms have become very successful. Tropical fruits are grown elsewhere in the selva.

(left) Banana farmers in the selva cut down big banana bunches and sell them at the markets.
(below) In the past, Inca farmers in the sierra used **terraces** *for farming. These terraces look like steps down the steep slopes. During heavy rains, they prevent soil from sliding down the mountain.*

 # Weaving—an ancient tradition

The **textile** industry, which includes the making of all types of woven cloth, is an important part of Peruvian life. Peru is famous for the colorful handmade cloth of the Native peoples who live in the mountains.

An ancient art

For centuries, textiles have been made by Native artisans. Ancient tapestries, which have been discovered in Nasca, Moche, and Inca tombs, can be seen in museums. Some of these colorful cloths show fanciful animals, intricate geometric designs, and gods in battle.

Weaving

The ancient skill of weaving is still practiced in the mountains. Weavers, most of whom are women, spin the fleece from alpacas, llamas, and sheep into yarn. The yarn, which is dyed bright colors, is threaded onto a loom and woven into cloth. There are many different types of looms. The traditional **backstrap loom** has two main

beams. One beam is suspended from a pole or pegged to the ground. The other is held in front of the weaver by a strap around his or her waist. By moving back and forth, the weaver can change the position of the threads.

Traditional handicrafts

The bright, thick cloth woven by Peruvians is often made into traditional handicrafts. The *alforja* is a type of saddlebag. The *liclla* is a square shawl that women use to carry babies. Ponchos, jackets, and capes are among the other articles of clothing made from woven fabric. Weavers sell these colorful creations at local markets.

(top) This piece of woven cloth came from a Chimú tomb. Ancient textiles found in coastal areas are well preserved because of the dry weather.
(opposite page) Using a backstrap loom, a Native woman weaves fabric.
(opposite page, inset) Looms are fastened firmly to the ground so the fabric can be woven tightly.

Transportation

The landscape of Peru makes traveling from place to place difficult. For example, to get from Lima to the jungle city of Iquitos, a traveler must cross mountains and large areas of dense rainforest. In the past, the easiest way to make the journey was not to make it at all! Instead, travelers took a boat along the coast of South America to the Amazon River and headed inland. This journey took weeks. Today an airplane can make the trip in 90 minutes!

Riding the rails

There are not many railroads in Peru. It is difficult and expensive to build tracks in the mountains. Near the end of the nineteenth century, however, an American engineer named Henry Meiggs supervised the construction of a railroad from Lima to a city called La Oroya. It is the world's highest railway line! Tourists enjoy traveling this route by train because of the breathtaking views of mountains, valleys, and gorges. During portions of the journey, many travelers need oxygen masks because of the high altitude.

Other ways to travel

Flying is a convenient way to travel in Peru, but flights are too costly for many Peruvians. Most people travel from one place to another by car, bus, or truck. The Pan-American highway, which runs through North and South America, is one of the many roads that crisscross the costa. In other parts of Peru there are few good paved roads. Remote parts of the country cannot be reached by car or truck at all!

Rolling down the river

Many small towns in the selva can be reached only by boat. If you were to take a voyage down one of Peru's tropical rivers, you would see a variety of vessels, including modern tourist boats, old cargo ships, and traditional dugout canoes.

(above) Dugout canoes are carved from a single log.
(opposite page) Roads in Peru's sierra wind up and down the steep slopes of the Andes.
(opposite page, inset) In Peru's countryside, villagers and farmers still rely on centuries-old transportation methods. They ride horses and donkeys or walk. Llamas and alpacas are used to transport goods from place to place.

Lost cities and ancient mysteries

A great deal is still unknown about Peru's ancient cultures. Many of the buildings and structures created by these peoples are mysteries that baffle the experts who study them.

The fortress of Sacsayhuamán
The enormous fortress of Sacsayhuamán covers an entire hill in the Cusco Valley. This earthquake-proof fortress is made of massive stone blocks, which weigh up to 200,000 kilograms (200 tons) each. The blocks were placed next to each other without mortar or cement. They fit together so tightly that not even a piece of paper can slide between them! The stone that was used to build the fortress was taken from a nearby quarry.

When the Spaniards first saw Sacsayhuamán, they thought it was so perfect that it could have been built only by the devil!

The legend of Vilcabamba
After the Spaniards came in 1532, some Incas fought for another 40 years from a rugged mountain stronghold called Vilcabamba. In 1911, a young explorer named Hiram Bingham was taken by local Natives to an unknown Inca city covered in forest, which they called Machu Picchu. Bingham thought these ruins might be the city of Vilcabamba. Today, experts do not believe Machu Picchu was Vilcabamba. They believe that Vilcabamba is closer to the rainforest.

Archaeologists are amazed by the skill of the workers who built the fortress of Sacsayhuamán. Artisans carefully carved each stone using hammers and chisels.

The candlestick of the Andes

A 250-meter (800-foot)-long "candlestick" carved into a cliff in the Andes Mountains is another of Peru's many ancient mysteries. No one knows the purpose of the candlestick or which culture was responsible for its creation. When the Spanish arrived in South America, they thought the candlestick was a sign from God telling them to conquer Peru.

Today some scientists believe that the candlestick may have been used as a calendar for predicting the ocean tides. Others think it was a giant **seismograph**—a tool used for measuring earthquakes. Treasure-hunters believe the candlestick is a marker meant to scare people away from a treasure buried nearby. An Inca legend states that the candlestick is actually the shadow of the god Viracocha, who once stood near that cliff with his arms outstretched.

The mystery of the Nasca lines

Etched into the desert outside the village of Nasca are mysterious animal shapes and straight lines that are several kilometers in length. The complete shapes can only be seen from the sky. A few people think that the Nascas may have used a type of hang glider or hot-air balloon for viewing the lines!

No one knows the purpose of these shapes and lines, but scientists have many theories. The most popular theory is that the animal shapes represent groups of stars, or **constellations**. The straight lines form a calendar that was used by farmers to keep track of the planting season. Other experts believe that Native peoples walked around the outlines of the animals to take on their powers.

(top) Carved into a cliff in the Andes Mountains, the "candlestick" can be seen from 20 kilometers (12 miles) away! The purpose of this enormous landmark is a puzzle for archaeologists.
(right) The "spider" is one of the many shapes etched into the desert near Nasca.

Natural wonders of Peru

Lake Titicaca

Lake Titicaca, located high in the Altiplano region of the Andes, is one of Peru's wonders. It lies on the border between Peru and Bolivia. Lake Titicaca is the highest lake in the world on which large ships are able to sail. Long before Europeans arrived in South America, the Native people of Lake Titicaca traveled the waters in reed boats called *balsas*. These reed boats are still used today!

The Colca Canyon

The Colca Canyon is the deepest gorge on earth. In some places it is 3.2 kilometers (2 miles) deep! The canyon is the result of millions of years of erosion, as the roaring Colca River carved a deep pathway between the mountains. Although it is not far from the city of Arequipa, few people visit this amazing sight. The area is so rugged that no road reached the gorge until 1970.

The Paracas Reserve

The Paracas National Reserve, established in 1975, is located on the coast of Peru near the city of Ica. The landscape of the reserve is rugged; the rocky coast is hit by strong winds and crashing waves. This area, however, is home to many marine animals, including sea turtles, otters, dolphins, sea lions, and many varieties of seabirds.

The beginnings of the Amazon

The place where a river begins is called its **source**. The Amazon River, one of the world's largest rivers, has several sources in the Peruvian Andes. The Apurímac River, for example, descends from an alpine lake near the Bolivian border. The river flows through the mountains and eventually reaches the selva. There, it joins a tropical river called the Ucayali, which flows into the Amazon. Every year, the Amazon rises and floods the lowland areas of the rainforest.

(top) This mountain stream is one of many that flow into the Apurímac River in southern Peru. The Apurímac eventually joins the Amazon River, which runs through Brazil to the Atlantic Ocean.
(inset) Orchids are beautiful, colorful flowers that can be found all over the world. Over 1300 species of orchids grow in Peru's rainforests.
(above) The rocky shore of the Paracas National Reserve is a refuge for Humboldt penguins.

(above) Llamas have excellent eyesight. Although it looks as if they are posing for a picture, they are probably keeping an eye on the human with the camera.

(above) Vicuñas have beautiful, fine wool. In the days of the Incas, only Inca royalty was allowed to wear robes made of vicuña fleece.

Llama-rama! 🦙

The llama is an important symbol of Peru. For thousands of years, the Native peoples of the Andes have relied on this animal in much the same way that the Native North Americans of the plains relied on the bison. Llamas are often used to carry loads from mountain farms to the local market. Dried llama droppings are collected and burned as fuel. Llama fleece is cut off when it grows long. It is spun into yarn, dyed, and woven into beautiful, colorful fabric. When a Native family butchers a llama, they eat its meat, use its fat to make candles, and cure and dry its skin to make leather sandals or bags.

Is that a llama?
The word "llama" is used to refer to four different animals. The common llama is a domesticated animal. It is raised by people. **Alpacas** are also domesticated. They have longer hair than llamas. **Guanacos** are similar to llamas, but they live in the wild.

The baby of the family
Vicuñas are the smallest member of the llama family. These cinnamon-colored animals live in the wild, high in mountain areas. In the past, hunters killed vicuñas in order to get their fleece, which is very fine and soft. Fortunately, vicuñas are now protected in Peru, and their numbers are growing.

Cousin to the camel
If you look at the face of a llama, you might notice a resemblance to the camel. Although these animals live in different parts of the world, llamas and camels are so similar that scientists say that they belong to the same animal family, *camelidae*.

(left) Llamas are used to carry goods to the marketplace. If a llama feels a load is too heavy, watch out! It will bite, kick, and even spit!

🦙 Glossary 🦙

alpine Describing or relating to high mountains

altitude The height of the earth's surface above sea level

artifact An old object that shows human craftsworking skill

artisan A person skilled in a craft

avalanche The sudden fall of a mass of snow, ice, earth, mud, or rocks down a mountainside

bison An animal found in North America and Europe, resembling an ox and having a brown coat and short, curved horns. It is also known as the buffalo.

bonito A saltwater fish related to the tuna and mackerel, found mainly in tropical seas

bribe A payment or gift used to influence a person's actions

civilization A society that achieves a great deal in the arts and sciences

condor A very large black-and-white bird of prey found in the mountains of California and South America

dune A mound of slowly shifting sand on a beach or in a desert

ecosystem Living things that are connected to one another in a particular environment

empire A group of countries or territories having the same ruler or government

engineer An individual who designs bridges, buildings, and other structures

erosion The gradual wearing away of soil and rock caused by wind or fast-moving water

evaporate To change from a liquid to a gas. Clouds and mists are evaporated water.

extinct No longer in existence; not seen in the wild for over 50 years

fertile Producing or able to produce abundant crops or vegetation

fertilizer A material added to the soil to make it produce more crops

glacier A large ice mass formed in areas where snowfall is greater than the amount that melts

gorge A deep, narrow opening between steep mountains or rock walls

habitat The natural environment of a plant or animal

irrigation Bringing water to land with a system of channels, pipes, or streams

livestock Domestic animals, such as cattle, horses, sheep, or pigs

mahogany A tropical evergreen tree with hard, reddish wood

manganese A metal used in the production of steel

mortar A soft building material used for binding bricks or stones together

plateau A flat, high-altitude plain

prospector A person who searches for gold

republic A democratic system of government in which the citizens elect a president

reserve Land set aside to protect an ecosystem

Roman Catholic Relating to the organization of Christians that is headed by the pope

rural Describing or relating to the countryside

saddlebag A bag made of leather or other material, usually one of a pair hanging from a saddle

Sahara Desert The world's largest hot desert, located in the northern part of Africa

shantytown A community in which the homes are simple shacks

sloth A slow-moving, tree-dwelling mammal that lives in the tropical forests of Central and South America

smallpox A highly infectious disease caused by a virus, often resulting in death

tapestry A heavy woven fabric decorated with designs or pictures

tapir A large, piglike animal that sleeps during the day and is active at night

☙ Index ☙

agriculture 5, 9, 10, 11, 14, 15, 21, 25, 27
Altiplano 13, 28
altitude sickness (*soroche*) 13
Amazon River 25, 29
ancient civilizations 6-7, 23, 26-27, 30
Andes Mountains 4, 11, 13, 14, 16, 19, 21, 25, 26, 27,
 29, 30
Apurímac River 29
archaeology 6, 7, 26, 27
architecture 6, 13, 26
Arequipa 28
Atahualpa 7
Atlantic Ocean 29
Ayacucho 7, 9
Bingham, Hiram 26
Bolívar, Simón 8
Callao 11
candlestick of the Andes 27
Chavín civilization 6
Chimú civilization 7, 23
climate 5, 11, 13, 14, 23
cloudforest 14
coastal region *See* costa region
Colca Canyon 28
Cordillera Blanca 13
costa region 6, 10-11, 13, 20, 21, 23, 25
crime 8, 9
Cusco 7, 13, 16, 26
drug trade 9
earthquakes 16, 17, 26, 27
economy 8, 9
El Misti 17
El Niño 11
farming *See* agriculture
fishing 11, 19, 20
foreign companies 8, 9
gold 19
guano 19
Huari civilization 7
Huáscar 7
Huascarán (mountain) 13, 17
Huascarán National Park 13
Humboldt Current 5, 11
Ica 6, 29
Inca civilization 4, 7, 8, 13, 16, 19, 20, 21, 23, 26, 27, 30

Iquitos 14, 25
Lake Titicaca 20, 28
Lima 8, 10, 11, 25
llamas 4, 13, 23, 25, 30
logging 14, 15, 18, 19
Machu Picchu 7, 26
Meiggs, Henry 25
minerals 18, 19
Moche civilization 6, 7, 23
Nasca civilization 6, 7, 23, 27
Nasca lines 6, 27
Native peoples 6-7, 8, 13, 14, 15, 18, 19, 20,
 21, 23, 26, 27, 28, 30
natural resources 8, 9, 18-19
oases 11
oil 14, 15, 18, 19
Pacific Ocean 11, 20
Pan-American highway 25
Paracas National Reserve 29
Pizarro, Francisco 7
plate tectonics 16, 17
railroads 25
rainforest 4, 5, 13, 14, 15, 18, 19, 21, 25, 26, 29
roads 6, 9, 25
rubber industry 14
Sacsayhuamán 26
San Martín, José de 8
selva region 11, 14-15, 19, 21, 25, 29
shantytown 10, 11
Shining Path 9
sierra region 11-12, 13, 14, 21
Spanish 4, 7, 8, 19, 20, 26, 27
terraces 21
terrorism 8, 9
textiles 23
tourism 9, 14, 15, 25
transportation 20, 24-25, 28
Tupac Amaru II 8
Ucayali River 29
Vilcabamba 26
volcanoes 16, 17
weaving 23, 30
wildlife 6, 11, 13, 14, 15, 19, 29, 30
Yagua people 15
Yungay 17

4 5 6 7 8 9 0 Printed in the USA 3 2 1 0 9 8